Brilliant Brain Selects Spelling Strategies

Ellen Arnold

Illustrations by Deborah Farber

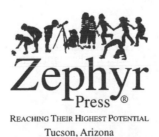

Zephyr
Press ®

REACHING THEIR HIGHEST POTENTIAL
Tucson, Arizona

Acknowledgments

—To Dick, whose smart parts are an endless inspiration—

Creating books takes work, but when you have a great team, the process can be joyful. Deborah Farber's picture smart part helped develop my ideas into a wonderful visual presence. Marti Arnold's word and number smart parts were an invaluable asset in helping me be clear, concise, and consistent. Without their patience, ideas, and support, this project would still be in my mind rather than in your hands.

Brilliant Brain Selects Spelling Strategies

Grades K–4

© 2000 by Ellen Arnold.

Printed in the United States of America

ISBN 1-56976-113-2

Editor: Bonnie Lewis
Design & Production: Daniel Miedaner
Cover Design: Daniel Miedaner
Illustrations: Deborah Farber

Published by
Zephyr Press
P.O. Box 66006
Tucson, Arizona 87528-6006
http://zephyrpress.com
http://giftsforteachers.com

Library of Congress Cataloging-in-Publication Data

Arnold, Ellen, 1944-
  Brilliant Brain selects spelling strategies / by Ellen Arnold ; illustrated by Deborah Farber.
    p. cm.
  ISBN 1-56976-113-2 (alk. paper)
    1   English language—Orthography and spelling—Study and teaching
    (Elementary)—Juvenile literature. 2. Multiple intelligences—Juvenile literature. 3.
    Learning strategies—Juvenile literature. [1. English language—Spelling. 2. Multiple
    Intelligences. 3. Learning strategies.] I. Farber, Deborah, ill. II. Title.

LB174 ,A75 2000
370.63'2044—dc21   00-033399

Brilliant Brain Selects Spelling Strategies

A Note to Teachers and Parents:

The key words Brilliant uses in this story are from the Dolch list and are words frequently misspelled by elementary students. **MI Strategies for Kids,** a teacher/parent manual, describes a lesson plan that will help make this book a most useful tool for the learner.

*B*rilliant Brain is a very smart thinking machine. But Brilliant struggles to spell. Other children just seem to know how to spell, but when Brilliant tries to spell words, he can't remember them very well. He feels frustrated.

*B*rilliant puts on his backpack and decides to visit his friends, the Smart Parts, who live inside his brilliant brain along, around, and through Intelligence Avenue. Maybe the Smart Parts can come up with more strategies to help him remember how to spell.

*F*irst Brilliant conducts a search for Music Smart. He uses Music Smart's language when he speaks.

4

BB: Music Smart, can you tell?
I am having trouble when I spell.
I say and practice every day
But many words refuse to stay.
The words don't stick inside my brain
It's like they all went down the drain.

MS: I'll try to help you figure out
What learning to spell is all about.
Spelling taps your memories,
How did you learn your 123's?
The ABC's came easy too,
because of songs we taught to you

BB: I am not sure I quite know how;
Can you help me practice now?
I'd like to store some words like "friend."
Is there a strategy you can lend?

MS: Take a song you know by heart
And that will show you where to start.

BB: Let's try *Twinkle, Twinkle Little Star*.
I know that one the best by far.
F-R-I, E-N-D, a friend is what I want to be.
F-R-I, E-N-D, my friend is always there for me.

MS: That's a great way to begin,
And soon the letters will sink in.

BB: Thanks, Music Smart. I like your trick—
It helped me learn this hard word quick.
Singing makes the letters flow,
This strategy builds words I know.

*A*nd Brilliant walked away,
singing his new song.

What is a word you
learned using your
music-smart part?

Sing the
Letters
Strategy

BB

*B*rilliant journeyed around Intelligence Avenue
until he sighted Picture Smart.

BB: Hi there. What are you picturing today?

PS: All kinds of things. You know how much I love pictures.

BB: Well, can you think of ways to use pictures to help me with spelling? Spelling has been really hard for me this year.

PS: Sure, are you taking pictures of the words?

BB: What? I don't think so. My teacher says to "sound them out," not take a picture of them. And my camera is all out of film.

PS: Yes, but you can take pictures of anything you want, develop them, and store them in your brain. Let's try it. What is a word you want to spell?

BB: How about *went*. That one is so confusing.

PS: OK. Let's put it in a picture. Do you remember what it means?

BB: Sure, it is like going somewhere.

PS: What does this shape look like to you?

BB: It kind of looks like a train. Could I add some wheels?

PS: Sure. Now make up a story about your picture.

BB: My train went for a ride to a magic land. My train went far. It *wandered every night till* it got to the magic land.

PS: Can you see it in your head, wandering? Close your eyes and look.

What is a word you learned to spell using your picture-smart part?

BB: I saw it clearly, Picture Smart. I saw the tall *t* at one end, pulling my little train as it **went** up this tall hill.

PS: Good for you. That's a great picture. I think it will help you spell. And remember, you have an unlimited supply of film to use any time you want to take a picture of something new.

BB: Wow! This is fun. I am going to add these pictures to my brain. Thanks for the "Take a Picture" strategy.

*H*mm, thought Brilliant. I wonder what Body Smart would do to learn words? So Brilliant bounced down Intelligence Avenue to Body Smart.

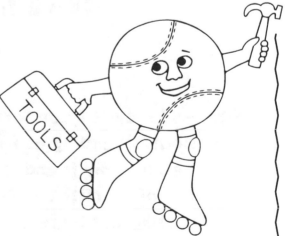

9

BB: Body Smart, can you help me tackle spelling?

BS: Sure, spelling is fun and easy as long as you **do** something to get the words to stick. I love to build things, and I can use letters instead of wood or pipe cleaners or blocks.

BB: How?

BS: Well, pick out a word, and we will build it together.

BB: How about *important*. That is a big, long word.

BS: Okay. Let's see if we can build something out of it. I'm going to take it apart.

im
port
ant

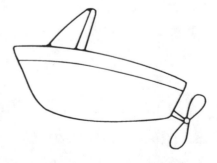

BB: And maybe I can take my toy boat over here. My boat is heading as fast as it can for the **port**, because my friend left his picnic basket there on top of an **ant** hill. Oops! It is really *important* that he get there before the ants take over, or he won't have any lunch left.

BS: Now scramble all the letters around and see if you can build the word.

BB: Wow, this is hard. I am not sure. But I do remember the **ant**, so I can pull those letters out, and I remember the boat is running back to **port**, so let's see if I can build that one. All I have left is the *i* and the *m*. I got it— **important.** That was fun!

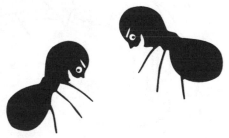

BS: Sure. I like to build words out of tiles, pipe cleaners, or just cubes I write letters on. I know if I can build or play with things when I learn, I can get the words to stick in my head.

BB: Thanks, Body Smart. I will add the "Build a Word" strategy to my strategy bank. I'll let you get back to your building.

What word can you spell using just your body to make the letters?

Build a Word Strategy

BB

BB: Oh, here is Self Smart. I don't want to interrupt, but I have a question.

SS: Yes . . . hmmm.

BB: Well, I know you think a lot, but have you ever thought about spelling?

SS: Sure. Sometimes. I think about lots of things.

BB: How do you feel about it?

SS: I think of spelling as a puzzle, a mystery, an unusual way for shapes and letters to appear.

BB: But have you thought of a way to really learn to spell? I get frustrated because I don't seem to be able to spell things right all the time.

SS: Maybe you are being hard on yourself. You don't have to spell right all the time. We have tools to help us check our spelling, like dictionaries, spelling machines, and computers. But I understand how you feel. I think about how one strategy won't work all the time for spelling. Think of it like a puzzle. Try to figure out a way that will work for you, word by word, so you can get the spelling to stick.

BB: That makes sense, but I am not sure how.

SS: What is a word you want to work on?

BB: Let's try *thought*. That word always seems to confuse me.

SS: Okay. That is a good one for me. First, think about what you already know.

BB: I know the *th* at the beginning. And I usually remember the *t* at the end. It is the middle stuff that gets all confused in my head.

SS: Think about what the rest of the letters remind you of.

BB: Well, they have some strange combinations. Like the *gh* part. That doesn't say anything, so it doesn't give me any clues.

SS: Well, maybe the *gh* likes to hide. Do you like to hide?

BB: Sure, sometimes. I like to hide outside. I love to play hide and seek with my friends.

SS: That's it. Look at the *gh*. They are hiding.

BB: Hey. That is cool. I can remember it like this: the **gh** are hiding **ou...t.** I like that!

SS: Sure, whenever you get stuck on a word, try to think about which parts you already know. Then think of something that will make it unique for you, something you can connect to. That way, the words will always be yours.

BB: Self Smart, you are soooo smart! I will put this idea in my strategy bank. Thanks.

What spelling word reminds you of something you already know?

What I Know Strategy

I don't think I could ever be as smart as all my Smart Part friends, thought Brilliant, as he roamed across the bridges of Intelligence Avenue.

WS: Never say *never*, Brilliant! You can be anything you want to be.

BB: **Oh, hi, Word Smart. I didn't know you were here. How do you know I can do it?**

WS: Because words are really fun. And once you get to know them, they can tell you their names.

BB: **What?**

WS: Try to think of the words that are inside other words. What words are connected to other words, or what do the words mean? I love to play with words.

BB: **How do you do that?**

WS: Well, take the word ***never.*** Are there any other words inside it?

BB: **Yes, "ever."**

WS: And what does *ever* mean?

BB: **It means all the time.**

WS: And what does ***never*** mean?

BB: **Not ever.**

WS: Sure, and the word **never** is just short for *not ever.*

BB: Do lots of words do that—take parts and push them together?

WS: Yes. And when you understand the smaller parts, you can learn the word more easily.

BB: Hmm. That is a really interesting way to do it. I will add the "Use Word Parts" strategy to my strategy bank. Thanks, Word Smart.

NS: 1, 2, 3, 4, 5, 6 …

BB: Oh, hi, Number Smart!

NS: What are you doing, what did you do before, and what are you going to do next?

BB: I am collecting ideas to put in my strategy bank to help me spell better. I have already asked some other Smart Parts, and I am trying to weigh the evidence to find out which strategies will work best for me.

NS: What have you learned so far?

BB: Well, so far I have learned five different ways. Each of the Smart Parts I have asked has given me another idea about ways to remember how to spell words. Do you have a way?

NS: Sure. I always get 100s on spelling tests. I love to figure out ways to learn words. One thing I do is to count the letters.

BB: Really. Why would you do that?

NS: Well, I remember numbers better than letters. So I count the letters. Like **really** has six letters. So when I think about **really equals six** I won't forget one. Because if I spell it just like it sounds, I might put in only four letters (r-e-l-y).

But knowing it has six letters helps me remember to add the ones I don't hear so that I have all the letters. Then I think really hard about **all** the letters that are supposed to be in the word.

BB: Oh, I figured it out. You found the word **all** in the word *really*.

NS: Sure, I add up the **all** and the sounds I hear and I am all set.

BB: So you make it into a math problem.

NS: Yep. Because for me, math problems are fun. So if I can make spelling into something I like, then I can have fun with it while I am learning.

BB: I like that idea. It sure adds up to a fun way to learn. Thanks, Number Smart. I'll add the "Count the Letters" strategy to my strategy bank.

Count the Letters Strategy

3-2x=y

BB

> *Think of a word you know that has eight letters in it. How about one that has nine letters?*

*B*rilliant went for a walk to think about all the things he had learned. He went to his favorite spot in the park and sat down under a tree.

NS: Hi, Brilliant. I haven't seen you here in a while.

BB: Hi, Nature Smart. I haven't been to visit in a while. I have been busy.

NS: Doing what?

BB: Trying to learn how to spell better.

NS: Well, did you think that I could help?

BB: No, I just came here to think. I didn't ask you because the trees, flowers, and animals don't have to spell.

NS: That's true, but all living things have patterns, and once you know about patterns you can know about spelling.

BB: I don't get it.

NS: Well, you are pretty good at remembering the signs for weather, aren't you? Like, do you remember how to tell if it is going to rain?

BB: Sure, you taught me to look at the sky, look for the changes in clouds, when the sun gets covered, and whether the wind changes direction or blows harder.

NS: Well, all those clues are part of a pattern. When the clouds get thicker, you can expect the winds to change. When the winds change, you can expect the weather to change.

BB: But what does this have to do with spelling?

NS: Look for patterns, Brilliant. Look for things that give you clues.

BB: Can we do an example? I'm not sure I understand. Help me with the word **could**.

NS: **Could.** Okay. Do you remember how to spell some of it?

BB: Yes. I remember the **C** at the beginning and the **d** at the end. It is the middle that gets all mixed up.

NS: Okay. Let's look carefully at **oul**. Let's find other words that have the same pattern. Look through all the words in this book and see which ones have the same letters.

BB: I see some.

Would and **should**

have the same middle as

could.

NS: That's right. Now think about something in nature that would help you remember **oul**.

BB: *O, U, L . . . Oh, you el . . . Oh, you elephant, could you help me, would you help me, should you help me?*

NS: Now you have the idea.

BB: Oh, you elephant . . . . Oh, you elephant. I think I got it. Thanks, Nature Smart. I am going to pay more attention to patterns from now on. And I remember what you taught me about elephants. They have really good memories. I'll put the "Patterns from Animals" strategy in my strategy bank.

Think of a word that has an animal in it.

Patterns from Animals Strategy

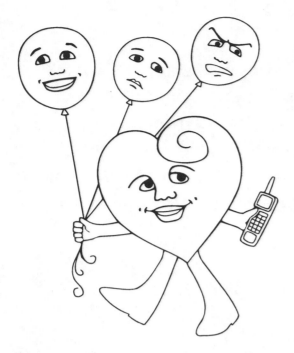

Brilliant wanted to share all the strategies he had learned with People Smart, who was playing with more friends at the playground.

PS: How are you doing today, Brilliant? It is good to see you. It has been a while.

BB: Well, yes. I have been kind of busy, trying to learn how to spell. I've been collecting strategies from the Smart Parts.

PS: Can we help you?

BB: I'd like to share what I have learned and see what you think. I'd just like to talk it out, okay? I can show you all the strategies I have in my strategy bank.

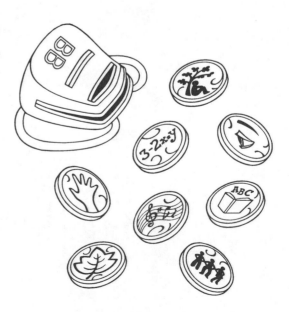

PS: Sure. We'll help in any way we can.

BB: First, from Music Smart, I got the "Sing the Letters" strategy with the letters of the word *friend*. It is fun to practice this strategy.

BB: Then, from Picture Smart, I got the "Take a Picture" strategy. I learned the word *went* by thinking of a train that went up the mountain. I can do pictures of anything I want!

BB: Body Smart taught me the "Build a Word" strategy. I can build words from all kinds of things. So I took a toy boat and took it into *port* to get the picnic basket off the *ant* hill, and that helped me to spell the word *important*.

BB: Self Smart gave me the "What I Know" strategy. I am supposed to think of what I know before I think about what is hard. Then I can connect it to something I do know. This one took some time, but I really learned how to spell the word *thought* this way.

BB: Word Smart gave me the "Use Word Parts" strategy. I can look for smaller words inside a word, or think about the meaning and how words fit together. I learned that *never* is a short form of *not ever*.

BB: Number Smart gave me the "Count the Letters" strategy. If I know how many letters are in the word, I can remember which ones are missing or how many letters are the same. I learned to spell *really* from Number Smart.

BB: The seventh strategy I learned was "Patterns from Animals." Nature Smart showed me how to find patterns and relate things to animals. I learned the word *could* using this strategy. And then I came to you.

PS: Because?

BB: Because you are my friend, too, and I wanted to find out if you had any ideas for me.

PS: It looks like your spelling strategy bank is getting pretty full. But I might have another strategy for you to try. I like to find people in my words. Give me a word to work on.

BB: How about *because*.

PS: *Because.* Well, how about breaking the word up into friends, like *be, ca, use.* We have a friend named Beatrice, but we always call her *Be.* She likes to dress up like a real bee and play pretend. When she was pretending to be a bee, she would *use* fake wings that her mother made for her. She would fly around the house, looking for flowers and honey. Her little sister loved to

watch her flap her wings, and would say *ca,* because she was too little and hadn't learned to talk yet. So if you think about *be* and *ca* and *use* you will get because. Now remember this advice. This is a special strategy to help you remember how to spell this word, but not how to read it.

BB: That's okay, People Smart. I have a different strategy bank for reading. But thank you for listening and sharing. I think your story about a real person helped me to remember **because.** And I will put my "Make a Story of a Real Person" in my strategy bank too.

Story of a Real Person Strategy

BB

*B*rilliant thought about what he had learned. He was very proud of himself. He had learned to spell eight different words that day. And they were hard ones, too. He **never thought** he **could** learn to spell, **because** he thought spelling was hard. It turned out that he liked spelling, if he had good strategies. Brilliant **went** to his **friends**, the Smart Parts, and each one gave him an **important** strategy that he could **really** use to make spelling easy.

*Y*ou see, Brilliant was brilliant after all. He could rely on all his smart parts for strategies to learn to spell. And when you use all your smart parts, you will be just as smart as Brilliant.